it comes to us all
– a portrait of Crookes Cemetery –

by Julie Stone

With research and photographs of the memorial inscriptions by Diane Gascoyne.

And personal contributions by the Gratton family, the Butterworth family, the Grogan family, Maureen Birch and Kay Paterson (nee Stead), Rene Lee (nee Foster), Vera Blow (nee Reaney), Ruby Widdowson (nee Greatbatch), Rita Kettlewell, Hazel Ansdell (nee Tyler), Pam Denniff (nee Frith), Thelma Johnson (nee Birchenough), and Doreen Stacey.

Photographs are reproduced from the author's collection and with the kind permission of the above contributors and Margaret Robinson for 'Crookes Revisited' and Gordon W Stone.

Acknowledgement is given to Sheffield Libraries Archives and Information; Local Studies for permission to reproduce images from their collection

and to Sheil Land Associates Ltd, for kind permission to reproduce the extract from 'Child of the War' by George MacBeth (published Jonathan Cape 1987).

Thanks to the staff of Sheffield Archives, Sheffield City Council Bereavement Services and Sheffield Local Studies Library, for their help and cooperation with research and illustrations.

Dedication
Dedicated to my mother Jessie Butterworth (nee Gratton) 1911-2004.

ISBN 0-901100-56-0

©Julie Stone 2004

con

Crookes Cemetery was the first establishe
This book looks at its history through the lives of the people who worked there as well as those who are buried there. It was the centre of life as well as death.

a part of our lives… living and working in and around the cemetery — 2
tells of Arthur Gratton's work as Cemetery Superintendent 1918–1948; his family living in The Lodge; the gravediggers; and the local children.

some practical issues… rules and regulations — 12
illustrated with reference to the family grave of Butterworth and the work of the monumental masons, and mention of presiding ministers and funeral directors

'where there is no vision the people perish'… a municipal cemetery with a spirit of unity — 22
the opening of the cemetery

from the memorial inscriptions… every grave tells a story — 25
the burials and memorials of some well-known Sheffield people, with newspaper reports, memorial inscriptions and photographs

after 'the war'… — 44
memories and photographs from local people of the 1940s and 1950s

approaching the centenary… — 47
Crookes is still a working cemetery and remains a part of the community

comprehensive index of surnames — 48

walkabout in the cemetery with map — 50

a part of our lives…

living and working
in and around the cemetery

In July 1919 Arthur Gratton, his wife Beatrice and two daughters Jessie and Ruth moved in to The Lodge at Crookes Cemetery. Little Jessie, aged eight years, was excited at the prospect of moving to a new house but the removal men were late and when the family eventually arrived it was dark and she thought it was a dreadful place. She imagined it would be like her Granny's farm in Fulwood and was very disappointed with what she found. Nor did it seem much better next morning but there *was* a lovely big field at the back to play in. Her sister Ruth was only a baby and Jessie had to look after her while her mother settled them into their new home.

The Lodge, built before the cemetery opened in 1910, was just within the gates at the top of Mulehouse Road and stood proudly overlooking the Rivelin Valley. High and exposed it had a lovely view. Jessie used to sit in the front window in the dusk and watch the lamplighter moving up the long road in the valley, lighting each gas lamp in turn. There was no electricity in the house and lighting was by gas. The mantels were very delicate and a steady hand was needed to put them in position, as a slight slip would cause damage.

There was a front room to be used for special occasions and a kitchen with its own fireplace but Beatrice's pride and joy was the big Yorkshire range in the living room. It provided the hot water, cooking facilities and heat. She would get up at 6.30am on Friday mornings to polish it. The iron bars were black leaded before lighting the coal fire. While it was burning up, the steel was cleaned with emery paper to remove any marks and then polished with Brasso mixed with Bath brick until it shone.

Upstairs were three bedrooms and opposite the top of the stairs a room with a bath and hot and cold water. The Yorkshire range had a back boiler to heat the water that was then stored in the cylinder in the corner of the room.

When it was bath night Beatrice would stoke up the fire to get the water hot. When bubbling could be heard it was time for the baths to begin. A water closet toilet was outside the back door.

The Lodge was provided rent-free together with a supply of gas and coal and was a big change for Beatrice from their previous home in Fitzmaurice Road.

The Lodge seen here in the 1950s showing the Cemetery Information Board on the house wall (with kind permission of the Grogan family)

the Superintendent

Arthur Gratton had moved to the Lodge to take up his post as sexton in Crookes, the first municipal cemetery in Sheffield.

On leaving school he had briefly followed his father in the cutlery trade but soon found it was not for him. He found himself a job as a groom's assistant at Bramley Hall, Handsworth. He then worked for the Firth family at 'Oakbrook' on Fulwood Road in Ranmoor. When Mark Firth moved to Ashwicke Hall in Gloucestershire the servants and gardeners were given the option of going with him. Arthur chose to go and there he lived in the 'bothy' with other young men on the estate and learnt much about gardening. One of these young men was Bob Foster with whom Arthur became close friends.

Ashwicke Hall, Gloucestershire (author's collection)

A bad bout of fever brought Arthur back to Sheffield and in the 1901 census members of his family were listed as gardeners (not domestic). Arthur began work for Sheffield Corporation in Hillsborough Park, tending the grass and creating displays of bedding plants.

In 1910 he married Beatrice Mills at All Saints, Fulwood and they moved to Fitzmaurice Road, Darnall, so that Arthur could go to his new job as a gardener in Tinsley Park Cemetery.

Tinsley Park Cemetery was consecrated by the Archbishop of York in 1882. There were two mortuary chapels. Mr J Bingham, Superintendent, resided on the premises.

When Attercliffe Cemetery was nearly full the Attercliffe Burial Board bought land from Earl Fitzwilliam in Tinsley Park Wood for a new cemetery. To cover the cost of the land, the fencing and the chapels, the Board borrowed £7,000 on security of the poor rates of the township.

The main entrance of Tinsley Park Cemetery (Gordon W Stone 2004)

Arthur Gratton and his wife Beatrice (nee Mills) with their daughter Jessie (author's collection)

Arthur and Beatrice's daughter, Jessie, was born in 1911 and in 1912 they proudly had their photograph taken in the garden of Mr Pratt, the chemist, in Darnall.

In 1914 World War I broke out. Gradually the existing gravediggers in the cemetery enlisted and Arthur, aged thirty-six, was asked to take over the job of digging graves. Although he had his calling-up papers, wartime brought many deaths and his services were needed in the cemetery.

By 1918 the war was over but the soldiers returning from the war brought an epidemic of Asian 'flu. People were dying 'like flies'. Arthur had to work day and night digging graves. Every day after school, little Jessie aged only seven, went from Fitzmaurice Road over wasteland to the cemetery to take her father his tea. It was November and there was no street lighting. It was pitch dark. She had to look among the graves until she found him digging by the light of a lantern.

In 1919 Arthur was asked whether he wanted to train for Superintendent at Crookes Cemetery. Arthur had left Greystones Elementary School at eleven but had reached a fair standard and was now keen to improve himself. He went every day for three months from Tinsley to Crookes to be trained.

Crookes Cemetery off Lydgate Lane comprised of 30 acres. The stone chapel had seats for 150 people. This Corporation cemetery was formed in 1910 and the foundation stone was laid in 1908 by the Lord Mayor (Alderman Harry Parker Marsh).

Arthur had to learn the layout of the cemetery and how to deal with burials. He was also required to know how to take money and keep accounts. He was a willing and conscientious pupil. Mr Cook was the Superintendent and arranged Arthur's training. When this was complete Arthur became sexton, the officer charged with the care of the chapel and the burial ground, with responsibility for the gravedigging. Mr Stephenson, the previous sexton, and his family had lived at The Lodge. He was to receive promotion and move to City Road so his family moved out and the Gratton family moved in.

Arthur was sexton until he took over as Superintendent in 1931. Mr Cook came every Friday to meet with Arthur and see that everything was running smoothly.

Arthur and Beatrice had two sons Edward and Dennis, born at the Lodge in 1921 and 1923 and all four children grew up living in the Lodge and going through the cemetery to Lydgate School every day. They played in the yard and orchard behind the house. The boys played football in the nearby fields.

Arthur in his allotment (author's collection)

Much of the land allocated for the cemetery was not needed immediately and was used as allotments for the local people. Arthur was provided with one, across the path opposite the Lodge. Here he grew cabbages and potatoes, chrysanthemums, rhubarb and dahlias and other fruit and vegetables to take home for his family. There was no shed or greenhouse in this allotment. The boys helped their father and carried the tools, when they were needed, from the shed at the back of the house.

The importance of gardening and allotments in the lives of the local people in the 1920s and 1930s is illustrated in the address of the Rev Cameron P Newell of St Thomas' Church (May 1933). He refers to those who have gardens and allotments finding plenty to do, getting busy digging and planting and comparing experiences about backache and seed potatoes. He then asks about the other allotment in the garden of our hearts. He goes on to use the analogy of gardening to preach his message.

the office and the burial register

Arthur's office was at the back of and adjoining the chapel.

The office was open from nine in the morning to five at night through the week. He was responsible for arranging funerals and for keeping the burial books, which were laid out on the desk – huge big ledgers with all the plots numbered. People could buy a plot when they needed it or before and when it was taken a big cross was entered in the ledger.

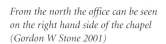

From the north the office can be seen on the right hand side of the chapel (Gordon W Stone 2001)

Arthur on the path outside the office (author's collection)

The Burial Register (with kind permission of Sheffield Archives and Sheffield City Council Bereavement Services)

The Burial Register contains the number of the entry, the number in the order book, the name of the person buried and a description of the person buried and their age, and the place where the death occurred, the date of burial and from which parish removed, the number of the grave and the section and in which part of the ground interred, the signature of the registrar and a column for remarks which gives further directions to finding the grave.

Arthur's neat signature confirms each burial.

The main entrance at Headland Road prior to completion of the cemetery (from 'Crookes Revisited' courtesy of Mrs D Hunt)

People used to call at The Lodge when they were wanting the office which was at the other end of the cemetery and Arthur's wife would send them off to find him in the office or out in the grounds inspecting the graves.

Arthur was now responsible for the security of the cemetery. He had the keys for three sets of gates: those at the Headland Road entrance, the outer gates at the top of Mulehouse Road, and the inner gate to the cemetery itself. He had to ensure that they were locked every night. The Mulehouse Road entrance gates were always kept locked except for special occasions but there was a pedestrian right of way through to Marsh Lane. Funeral corteges used Headland Road entrance to arrive at the chapel. Every night at closing time the big gates would be locked. The stone gateposts had conical top pieces which were removed when they were found to be unsafe in 1983.

the local children

The main drive through the cemetery was well used by local people. Vera Blow (nee Reaney) remembers walking to Lydgate School and back every day in the 1920s. From Toftwood Cottages, at the top of Toftwood Road, she would go through into Stannington View Road then turn right and follow the unmade road round to come out in Mulehouse Road on the corner by the shop and opposite the stonemason's workshop. She would then go through the gates and pass the Lodge, through the smaller gates and along the main drive until she reached Headland Road. The children were all going to school at the same time and would meet up with each other and chatter as they went. Vera remembers Ruth Gratton from school. The children were well-behaved and so they were never stopped from being in the cemetery even if there was a funeral.

In the 1920s Headland Road was still rural with few houses. As the children went on to school in Lydgate Lane they passed the pasture fields belonging to Elliot's farm on the left hand side of the road. On the right hand side there were just a couple of houses and next to the cemetery the premises of S Hancock and Sons, monumental mason.

Herbert Tyler took over these premises around 1930 and brought up his family. New houses were built on Headland Road and more children came to live there. His daughter Hazel (Ansdell) remembers how they used to play in the cemetery after the gates were closed. She and her friend Pam (Denniff nee Frith) would take a bucket of water and wash the gravestones to clean them up. They would put flowers on the ones that were neglected. At dusk when no one was about, they would use the stone steps opposite the chapel as an impromptu stage to hold their concerts. There were 'special' graves with angels and cherubs and they used to sit by them and tell stories and wonder about them. They knew that children were not allowed in the cemetery really but they had been taught to take care of the place. Pam remembers that when she saw her first funeral she didn't know what it was and thought it was a May Queen procession. Her mother had to explain and teach her respect.

The children never had any fear of the cemetery. It was a peaceful and safe place. Rita Kettlewell remembers hearing that a little boy from Salisbury Road was missing one day and when he was eventually found he said he had been to talk to his angel.

The route to school from lower down Mulehouse Road would not be through the cemetery. The children would turn on Cross Lane and then cut across Sanderson's field diagonally to come into the jennel that led on to Lydgate Lane.

Dennis Gratton remembers how the children, as well as the gravediggers and workmen, would climb over the boundary wall of the cemetery to take a short cut through to Crosspool. In later years houses were built and the shortcut was no longer possible.

Arthur was also responsible for the appearance of the cemetery. His gardening skills were needed to ensure that the grass was cut and the flowerbeds were bright with bedding plants. He took pride in knowing the Latin names and in teaching young Jessie to repeat them. The grass grew long in places and provided a playground for the children. When it was hay making time men would come from Sanderson's farm to collect the cut grass and the children would help to collect it up and load the cart.

the gravediggers

Four gravediggers were employed who also looked after the gardens. In the corner by the wall at the Headland Road entrance was a lovely big greenhouse

Scything the grass in the top field with Mod Bingham on the left (with kind permission of Doreen Stacey)

with a fire and a chimney and the workmen had their dinner in there. Here the bedding plants for the flowerbeds were raised. In later years this top corner behind the greenhouse became a favourite courting spot for the young people including Arthur's son Ted.

In the 1920s Arthur's daughter Jessie remembered the gravediggers.

Joe Twigge, lived at Wyming Brook by the water. He had a daughter and young Jessie used to go and stay. Some years later when Mr and Mrs Twigge lived with their daughter in Lodge Lane, Arthur used to take his sons Ted and Dennis to visit on Sunday mornings. Mrs Twigge used to give the boys a drink of milk. Joe used to walk to work every day from Lodge Lane.

Jim Lister was older and lived at Ringinglow. He was retired from gravedigging but still did the gardens. He too used to walk to work. He used to call at the Lodge for his tea to be mashed.

George Stead worked in the cemetery for fifty years and lived at Stephen Hill Cottages opposite the top of Benty Lane. He also walked to work and back every day and his weathered skin reflected the years of working outdoors in all weathers. His granddaughter, Maureen, remembers her nan packing up his sandwiches and then she would take them to the cemetery using the short cut over the wall in Marsh Lane.

George was a 'bit of a lad' and liked a drink of beer in *The Sportsman* on Manchester Road. His family had been publicans in Crookes for many years, keeping the *Original Grindstone* on Crookes when George was young.

Sadly two of his sons died in the 'flu epidemic and another in a tragic accident in North Africa. After George Stead retired from gravedigging, his niece Kay Paterson (nee Stead) remembers how much fun he was, how he used to make the children laugh. He could always provide and 'make-do' for their games.

Ready for a day's outing outside the Crosspool Tavern. Days off were well spent after a hard week's work in the cemetery (with kind permission of Maureen Birch)

Smiles all round on a good night out in The Sportsman on Manchester Road – George Stead in the hat with white silk scarf and the buttonhole he always wore (with kind permission of Maureen Birch)

Then there was Motson (Mod) Bingham who lived in Fulwood. He was younger than the others and was glad to get a job in the cemetery as times were hard and he had been out of work. He was cousin to Beatrice, wife of Arthur Gratton. His mother Caroline (nee Comins) was sister to Beatrice's mother, Julia. Caroline and Julia's mother was a Motson and the family came from Lincolnshire. Motson lived with his wife, Marion and their seven children in a small cottage in Chorley Road with one room, a small kitchen, two bedrooms and an attic. The family attended Fulwood Church as did Beatrice and her family and the children went to the Church School.

From October 1946 M Bingham signed the Burial Register until Michael Grogan took over in December 1947.

Motson died in 1959, aged seventy-five, and is buried in the cemetery.

Jessie Gratton and her sister Ruth outside the Lodge in the 1930s (author's collection)

the Superintendent's family

Arthur and Beattie's family were growing up.

In 1937 Jessie married George William Butterworth at St Thomas' Church and held a reception tea at the Baptist Chapel Hall in Mulehouse Road. They moved into a little house at the top of Newent Lane. These were happy days before the threat of war.

World War II meant Arthur's sons and son-in-law joined up, into the Army and the Royal Air Force. Arthur was exempt and continued with his work in the cemetery. Harry Frith, along with other older men from Headland Road, assisted the Air Raid Precautions by firewatching in the cemetery. In the dark, and even the snow, Pam and her mother used to take tea for the men on duty and find them sitting on the first bench inside the gates. Herbert Tyler as a member of the Auxiliary Fire Service had to report to the fire station whenever there was a raid.

On the night of the 'blitz' a bomb landed at the top end of the cemetery by the greenhouse and Herbert Tyler's showroom window was blown out. Another bomb dropped but remained unexploded and the police closed off the area and would not let people in even though there was a funeral. Arthur insisted on going into the office in spite of the risk.

By the end of World War II Arthur was sixty-seven and past retiring age. He had stayed on, as there was no one to take over until the servicemen returned.

On 21 September 1946 a letter from Mr E O Sadler manager of the Municipal Parks, Cemeteries and Allotments Department, thanked Arthur for delaying his retirement beyond the official retirement age and recorded the Committee's appreciation of his long years of service.

It was a skilled job managing the cemetery. Care had to be taken to ensure the graves were safe. Part of the cemetery, on the bank opposite the chapel used to get water logged in bad weather. The winds blew hard and

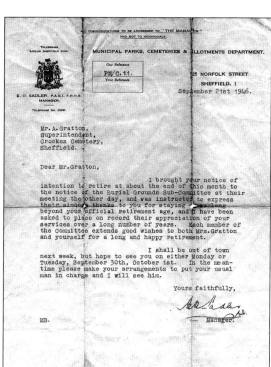

The letter of appreciation to Arthur Gratton on his retirement from Sheffield Corporation Burial Grounds Sub-Committee 1946 (author's collection)

Arthur on the steps opposite the chapel in the snow of 1947 (author's collection)

the rain and snow swept across the valley. Pam Denniff remembers helping dig out the hearses when they became stuck in the snow on Headland Road. In 1947, before Arthur was able to retire, there was a really deep snowfall but he and the men had to keep the paths open. Funerals do not wait for good weather.

Eventually Arthur's sons and son-in-law returned from their wartime service. His youngest son Dennis came home to The Lodge. His son Ted left The Lodge when he married. Jessie's home in Newent Lane had been bombed but with George back she was now resettled. There were more happy times.

The wedding of Ruth Gratton at St Thomas' Church in 1947 (author Julie in poke bonnet) (author's collection)

In 1947 Arthur's daughter Ruth was married from the Lodge to John Ballington.

and retirement

Whilst Arthur worked in the cemetery he was responsible for more than 8,000 burials. Now aged sixty-nine he was able to retire.

Mr Michael Grogan became Superintendent. He was an Irish ex-army man who was a qualified blacksmith, farrier and wheelwright. He had worked at Shiregreen Cemetery before and after World War II. He and his family moved into The Lodge in Christmas week 1947.

Arthur and Beatrice and Dennis moved out of the Lodge into a house provided by the Corporation. The furniture was moved and one of the

The wedding guests at the back of The Lodge – Arthur Gratton next to daughter Jessie and from left to right sons Dennis and Edward and on the front row sons-in-law John and George (author's collection)

gravediggers, Lou Foster from Bole Hill Lane, brought his pony and cart to transport the garden shed (home of all the garden tools for the allotment) from the back of The Lodge. The shed was so heavy that the pony was nearly lifted off the ground!

Arthur had to give up his allotment when he moved but he took over the one with the greenhouse next to the one he had had for many years. He used to walk every day from Heavygate Road to the cemetery to tend his patch and grew some very tasty tomatoes.

Sadly Beatrice died in 1954 and although severe storms battered his house in 1961 and Arthur had to move out, he lived until he was ninety-four years going for a walk every day and enjoying a pipe of 'baccy'.

After many years of digging graves he did not want to be buried but was cremated on 29 August 1973 and his ashes placed on his wife's grave. The stonemason was Walter Hoyland from Headland Road, a good friend of Arthur.

The bride's mother Beatrice, and on the left her sister-in-law Eileen, in the yard behind The Lodge (author's collection)

Arthur Gratton aged ninety-one years, outside Parkhead House, Whirlow (Dennis Gratton 1969)

In Loving Memory of
BEATRICE
Beloved wife of Arthur Gratton
Died Oct 9TH 1954 aged 71 years
Also Arthur
Loving husband of Beatrice
Died Aug 29TH 1973 aged 94 years
Reunited

*The Gratton grave
(Gordon W Stone
2002)*

some practical issues...
rules and regulations

Looking round the cemetery there are many stories to be told. A social as well as a family history is there for the finding – graves and memorials for the famous and the not so famous.

the purchase of a grave

Jessie Gratton married George William Butterworth, whose family had lived in Crookes for some years. George's grandfather, William Butterworth, a staunch Wesleyan Methodist,

The Butterworth grave 1928 (author's collection)

Purchase of exclusive rights of burial (author's collection)

purchased a grave for his wife in 1918 in the general portion of the cemetery only a few years after it was opened. The non-conformists did not want to be buried in the consecrated section. From the paperwork accompanying the burials together with the Rules and Regulations of the cemetery it is possible to trace the events pertaining to this grave as they took place.

On 22 April 1918 William Butterworth purchased the grave No 2382 Section D with exclusive rights of burial at a cost of £3 17s 0d.

A plan of the cemetery was available for inspection in the office behind the chapel between 9am and 5pm.

William would have consulted this plan and discussed his requirements with Mr Cook, the Superintendent. The position of the grave was an important decision. Account had to be taken of the prevailing winds and rain, the moisture level of the ground to allow for a four person depth as well as whether the section was consecrated for church members or general for non-conformists.

The costs are to be found in the *'Table of Fees and Payments for Crookes Cemetery'* fixed and settled by the Lord Mayor, Aldermen and Citizens of the City of Sheffield acting by the Council as the Burial Authority for the City of Sheffield (Section 34 of the Burial Act 1852).

William purchased a grave with exclusive rights of burial. Plots could be purchased without exclusive rights or with exclusive rights lasting for a limited period. In the Rules an interment with exclusive right of burial in perpetuity in an earthen grave nine feet by four feet, section D would cost £1 7s 0d. This was the standard size for a grave in Crookes Cemetery except for the marginal grave spaces, which were laid out at eight feet by four feet and were for public use only. During Arthur Gratton's first month signing the Burial Register, a still born child was buried without ceremony in a marginal section.

The Butterworth grave was to be dug to a depth of ten feet allowing for four burials. According to the Rules and Regulations of the cemetery when sites for graves were purchased for future use the purchaser had to erect good and substantial edge stones to define the grave, within twenty-eight days. The edge stones were required to be not less than nine inches deep and three inches thick and were to be fixed not less than three inches in the ground and according to the formation of the ground. The number of the grave according to the plan must be legibly engraved on the upper surface.

On 15 January 1919 William Butterworth paid £1 6s 0d for the right of interment of his wife Ellen. Mr C Cook was the Superintendent. Arthur Gratton had yet to take up his post as sexton.

Notice had to be given of the proposed interment between 9am and 5pm Monday to Saturday, at least two days beforehand. The ordinary hour for interment in the General Section was 2.30pm. By this time the procession must be in the cemetery. Penalties were imposed if the party was more than fifteen minutes late.

presiding ministers

Because Crookes Cemetery was a municipal one, open to all faiths, the burial service could be conducted by a minister chosen by the family of the deceased. In the Burial Register there are many ministers who officiated at the interments. Between 1906 and 1910 some thirty-four ministers presided over the burials, including Henry Martin of St Thomas' Church who together with C Ensor Walters of Wesley Hall, SM Bridge and John Francis Matthews and J Gascoyne conducted most of the ceremonies. The minister's fees were 2s 0d if the burial service was at the ordinary hour agreed in the Rules, 10s 0d if out of hours in the morning and 5s 0d if between 1pm and 2.30pm.

In 1918 when Arthur first went to Crookes, NF Duncan from St Thomas' Church and George R Ekins, Vicar of St Timothy's, SR Butterton from St Nathanael's, Crookesmoor (buried next to Sir Stuart Goodwin) and

W Norton Wright from St Stephen's, Crosspool conducted ceremonies in the consecrated section.

In the general part of the cemetery, GA Hillyar-Russ, Wesleyan Methodist and Charles Higgins, Primitive Methodist represented the non-conformists, together with FD Franks and BG Butt.

The families of Ellen and William were loyal supporters of the Wesleyan Methodist Church from the very early days when John Wesley came to Yorkshire. William worked as a town missionary in Hull, Normanton and London before he came to St John's, Crookesmoor. The minister who conducted the burial ceremony for Ellen was Frank Spencer.

interment

Before an interment could take place the certificate of ownership of the grave must be provided. The burial and the minister's fees must be paid to the Superintendent at the time notice of interment was given. When the funeral party entered the cemetery the death certificate or in cases of an inquest the Coroner's warrant must be handed to the Superintendent.

All graves had to be excavated by persons appointed by the Corporation. Masonry and brickwork was to be arranged by the purchaser but under the control of the Corporation. Arthur would have been responsible for the digging and management of the graves according to the Rules and Regulations.

If a headstone was to be erected it must be done within twelve months of the interment. All memorial inscriptions were subject to approval of the Corporation. A copy of the inscription and a drawing showing the dimensions of the headstone had to be submitted to the Superintendent's office at least fourteen days before its proposed erection. A certificate would be supplied and a copy of the same filed in the office for future reference. The grave number must be included on the memorial. William would have to arrange all of this.

the monumental masons

Monumental masons were at both ends of the cemetery.

At Headland Road gates in the 1920s were S Hancock and Sons, monumental masons, who also operated from Nethergreen Road. In the 1930s, Herbert Tyler, Hazel Ansdell's father occupied the premises. Herbert worked with Percy Evans. The headstones came ready cut to size and were of different measurements. Marble came from Italy until World War II stopped its importation. Other headstones were of Cornish granite.

Hazel and her friend Pam used to watch the men cutting inscriptions with mallet and chisel or drilling holes to secure the inserted lead lettering. The children used to play in the showroom where the headstones were on display.

After Herbert Tyler retired, through ill health, the business passed to Walter Ernest Hoyland of Bingham and Hoyland, who were based at 212 Tapton Hill Road. Dennis Gratton use to watch Walt in the workshop, where he cut huge slabs of stone using a blade hanging from the ceiling. He would throw water onto the stone to reduce friction and then push the blade along with his bodyweight.

The names of these masons can still be seen on graves in the cemetery.

At the other end of the cemetery on the corner of Stannington View Road and Mulehouse Road was Thomas Birchenough, monumental sculptor.

The stationery rubber stamp of T Birchenough (with kind permission of Thelma Johnson)

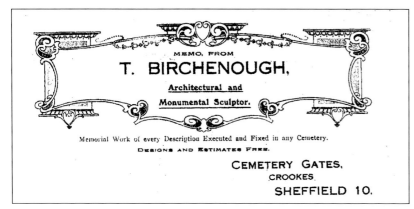

Headed notepaper for T Birchenough, architectural and monumental sculptor offering memorial work of every description (with kind permission of Thelma Johnson)

Christopher Harold (grandson of Thomas) and his family have found that Thomas was born in Manchester and descended from generations of stone carvers, sculptors and artists. Thomas was a master sculptor and the only one in Sheffield able to carve the Corinthian cornices on top of the pillars, which form the frontage of the City Hall but as the job was too big for him to undertake alone, stone carvers were brought in from Italy. He also taught his skills for two evenings a week at the Art College in Sheffield.

Thomas worked in his yard from the opening of the cemetery until his death in 1932 and passed his skills on to his son Thomas Harold, who continued after his father's death until ill-health forced his retirement in early 1940. Dennis Gratton remembers seeing a carved angel in the workshop yard behind their house.

The Butterworth headstone showing the work of T Birchenough including the 'carved hands' for which he was well-known (author's collection)

Thomas Harold Birchenough on the left in the workshop yard, Stannington View Road (with kind permission of Thelma Johnson)

Footstone showing the name of the mason and the number of the grave (author's collection)

For the right to erect and place a headstone not exceeding five feet in height William would have paid 2s 6d. All memorials had to be completed before being admitted to the cemetery and only fixing was allowed on site. The work had to be completed by Friday as no work was allowed on Saturdays.

There were clear instructions for the stonemasons. No Bath, Caen or other soft stone was to be used for memorials. Borders and edging were not to be made from concrete, cement, imitation stone, slate or any materials likely to perish or become unsightly. Brick foundations were required for monuments and headstones if the Superintendent deemed it necessary. Only copper cramps and dowels were allowed for the fixing of the memorial. Permission from the owner of the grave was required for the fixing to take place.

Whilst the majority of headstones in Crookes Cemetery are of plain design there are some more ornate examples to be found.

All materials, gravestones and monuments had to be brought into the cemetery by hand or on carts or trucks with wheels of not less than four-inch flat-surfaced tyres (to spread the weight and prevent making ruts in the ground) and between the hours of 9am and 2pm. All workmen must clear the cemetery by 5.30pm.

Next to The Lodge at the top of Mulehouse Road was Joseph Arthur Knowles' workshop. He cut stone from a small quarry at the back of the workshop abutting the cemetery wall. The tap-tapping of the stone cutting could be heard as people passed by. The stone supply eventually ran out and the workshop was closed and the quarry levelled in readiness for development. The Knowles family lived further down Mulehouse Road on Tasker Road. Young Jessie Gratton remembers playing with the son of the family. A man called Horace worked for Knowles and became friendly with Arthur.

Shrubs, plants or flowers planted over the purchased grave were subject to the approval of the Corporation and may not be cut and taken away. This was to prevent the removal of flowers by unauthorised persons. The Corporation reserved the right to prune, dig up or cut down any overgrown or unsightly plants. On payment of extra fees the Corporation would undertake to keep the grave space in order and provide planting.

In turf	5s 0d per year
Planted with mixture of herbaceous plants and annuals	7s 0d per year
Watering and attending to planted graves	5s 0d per year

On 28 August 1922 Frederick William Butterworth paid £2 9s 0d for the right of interment in the said grave and for the burial of his father William Butterworth. Mr C Cook was still the Superintendent. Rev CE James from St John's, Crookesmoor, was presiding minister.

Receipt for the burial of William Butterworth 1922 (author's collection)

In October 1922 when Arthur Gratton began signing the Burial Register he would have made arrangements with many different ministers, getting to know some of them well. NF Duncan from St Thomas' Church, SR Butterton from St Nathanael's and GR Ekins from St Timothy's presided over most of the burials in the consecrated section whilst FD Franks, JR Cooper and others continued to represent the non-conformist members of the population.

The Butterworth grave had been dug to a depth of ten feet when purchased at an extra cost of £1 10s 0d. After Ellen's burial the coffin would have been surrounded with earth and then sealed with wooden slabs and then refilled to the surface with earth. The purchaser was responsible for this action plus removal of any refuse and repair to any damage done to surrounding graves. For William's interment, the gravediggers would have to reopen the grave and dig out the earth until they reached the boards covering Ellen's coffin. After William had been lowered into the grave, earth would again be replaced around the coffin and more boards placed over the coffin and the remaining space refilled with earth until the site was level.

funeral arrangements

Sadly William's son, Fred, died aged only fifty-four, when he and his wife Ethel were on a day out in Derbyshire on their motorbike. He was buried in the family grave. On 15 May 1928 Emily E Butterworth paid £2 9s 0d for the right of interment of her husband Frederick William Butterworth.

The funeral was arranged by Maurice Smith, funeral director and coffin maker of 126 Howard Road, Walkley at a cost of £20 0s 0d. Because of his sudden death Fred's body had to be brought back from Hulme End, Derbyshire, a fact that is detailed in the Burial Register. The cortege consisted of a glass car and two carriages. There were four bearers who carried the oak coffin. An allowance was given to the drivers and the bearers.

During the hours of funerals the roads adjacent to the cemetery (that is Headland Road) were not to be used as a promenade. The children from Headland Road in the 1930s were taught to be respectful when a funeral was passing. Games were halted and the children stood still while the cortege passed.

Receipt for the burial of Frederick William Butterworth in 1928 signed across the postage stamp by A Gratton (author's collection)

Carriages and horses accompanying funerals were admitted into the cemetery as far as the chapel. Other vehicles were not admitted. The presiding minister at Frederick William's funeral was Rev NF Duncan from St Thomas' Church, Crookes and the Parish Magazine records his death under *Parish Notices 17 May 1928, 'If the Lord Will'*.

Emily Ethel, Frederick William's wife was buried with her husband and his parents on 2 January 1958. The sum of £5 7s 6d was paid: £4 0s 0d for the interment in an earthen grave or vault in respect of which an exclusive right of burial had been granted, 10s 0d for the minister and 17s 6d for mats and music.

William's daughter Caroline and her husband George Oxley were cremated but their names are remembered on the memorial inscriptions.

In Loving Memory of
Ellen
Beloved wife of
William Butterworth
Who died Jany 15th 1919 in her 81st year
'Faithful and True'
Also of the above named
William Butterworth
Who died Aug 28th 1922
In his 87th year
'to the weary he giveth rest'
Also Frederick William
Beloved husband of Ethel Butterworth
And son of the above
Who died May 13th 1928
Aged 54 years
'in the midst of life we are in death'
In memory of
George Harry Oxley
Beloved husband of Caroline Oxley
Born Jan 26th 1871 died May 15th 1953
Cremated May 20th 1953
Also of Emily Ethel Butterworth
Beloved wife of Frederick William
Died Dec 30th 1957
Aged 82 years
'reunited'

On a separate stone is recorded the death of

Caroline Oxley
The Beloved wife of George Harry
Died Jan 10th 1958 Aged 83 years.

The Butterworth headstone (Gordon W Stone 2002)

the cemetery rules

The Rules and Regulations and Fees of the cemetery were produced in 1910 and were freely available to clergymen, ministers of every denomination, churchwardens, overseers, clerks and sextons of the City. To all others a cost of 3d was charged. No gratuities were allowed to any employee of the Corporation.

The cover of the Rules and Regulations book 1910 (extract from Sheffield Local Studies Library material)

The reverse of a burial receipt showing 'Extracts from the Rules &c' (author's collection)

Extracts from the Rules are to be found on the reverse of the grave receipts.

These extracts reinforce the rules about the excavation of graves, the erection of memorials with their inscriptions and the keeping of the grave thereafter. Fees are listed and opening times of the cemetery.

> *Children under ten were not allowed in the cemetery without an adult. Visitors must use the paths and not touch the plants. Dogs were not allowed and there was to be no smoking.*
>
> *The cemetery was open to the public on weekdays:-*
> *in January, February, November and December from 9am to 4pm*
> *in May, June, July and August from 7am to 8pm*
> *in March, April, September and October from 7am to 7pm*
>
> *On Sundays opening times were:-*
> *in January, February, November and December from 10am to 4pm*
> *in May, June, July and August from 10am to 6pm*
> *and in March, April, September and October from 10am to 5pm*
>
> *The Register of Burials is kept at the Office of the Superintendent and may be searched between 9am and 5pm and certified extracts obtained except on Sundays and Bank Holidays.*

[The Register of Burials is now held on microfilm at Sheffield Archives Shoreham Street]

a hidden grave

A grave does not have to have a headstone to have a story. A turf covering belies the history of such a grave. Rita Kettlewell (nee Handley) is granddaughter of Alice and Jameson Lawton Firth of Mulehouse Road. Rita visited her grandmother in Mulehouse Road once a week in the 1940s.

Alice Firth (nee Kemp) died 4 March 1954 aged 80 years and was the last to be buried in this four-person grave. Rita remembers her saying "there's just room for me in there." According to the grave receipt it was in section DD a consecrated section of the cemetery when it was opened.

Receipt for the burial of Alice Firth 1954 (with kind permission of Rita Kettlewell)

In the 1950s Alice moved to live near her daughter who was a member of St Luke's Methodist Church and Rev Reginald T Wagstaffe conducted Alice's service in the cemetery chapel.

Jameson Lawton Firth attended St Thomas' Church, Crookes (known as low church) whilst Alice was a regular member of St Timothy's Church at the far end of Crookes (more of a high church).

Sadly in 1933 Jameson was knocked down by a bicycle on the corner of Mulehouse Road and Tasker Road age seventy-one and died from his injuries, leaving Alice a widow only sixty years old.

Rev Cameron P Newell of St Thomas' Church writes in the Parish Magazine:

Message of sympathy from Rev Cameron P Newell in the parish magazine of St Thomas' Crookes (with kind permission of Rita Kettlewell)

Notice of the burial is also given.

Notice of burial in the parish magazine (with kind permission of Rita Kettlewell)

Jameson Firth was the third person to be interred in the grave on 8 April 1933.

The grave was purchased by Thomas Kemp, Alice's father, for his wife Elizabeth who was buried 17 March 1913. Thomas and Elizabeth must have been church goers to choose a plot in the consecrated section (DD) of the cemetery. Their daughter Jessie married John Beevers but sadly she died in the great 'flu epidemic and was the next to be interred in the grave 30 November 1918.

Alice Firth used to go and sit in the cemetery after her husband died and always found it a very peaceful place.

From marble monument to grass turf every plot has its story – the lives as well as the deaths of families are fixed in remembrance.

'where there is no vision the people perish'…

a municipal cemetery with a spirit of unity

Crookes Cemetery was the first to be *established* by the Corporation. Other burial grounds were managed by the Corporation since about 1900 but were originally controlled by the old Burial Boards.

There had been urgent need for a new cemetery in Crookes. The old churchyard at St Thomas' had been full for some six years and the population of the parish was now 20,000. The Vicar of Crookes told of a burial taking place only feet from the cellar wall of the adjoining house.

the opening ceremony

On **Friday 18 September 1908** at 12.30pm the Lord Mayor, Alderman Harry P Marsh JP, laid the foundation stone of the new municipal mortuary chapel. He was then presented with a silver trowel by the architects, Messrs C and CM Hadfield. Various religious organisations were represented and many councillors and members of the general public attended the ceremony.

Alderman George Senior JP, Chairman of the General Purposes and Parks Committee, took the chair and told of the lengthy hunt there had been to find a suitable site. The twenty-eight acres cost £350 per acre. It was therefore most suitable and cheap. It was clear of rock and free of water, two very important factors in making a cemetery. Those built on the hills being full of rock and those in the valleys full of water. Alderman Senior still retained the old fashioned prejudice against cremation.

Councillor J Knowles JP, chairman of the Burial Grounds Sub-Committee, expected the expenditure on the whole scheme to be £21,000 but they were not proposing to lay out the whole cemetery at present. A large proportion had been handed over to the Allotments Committee for letting out in small plots. Unemployed men laid out the main road through the cemetery during the winter of 1907.

Alderman Marsh did not believe in expensive funerals. He said, "I hope the funerals held here will be simple and inexpensive. Funerals are often made much too costly. Rich people set the example and their poorer brethren think they must spend the whole of the money they draw out of the clubs on such occasions, whereas it would be much better saved." He also believed it was better for the funeral services to be held in the church or chapel and for only the immediate family to come to the cemetery.

Alderman Harry Marsh laying the foundation stone of the chapel, Crookes Cemetery (Sheffield Daily Telegraph 19 September 1908) © Sheffield Libraries, Archives and Information; Local Studies

Rev Henry Martin vicar of St Thomas' Church on the right and beside him Rev C Ensor Walters, Wesleyan minister (Sheffield Daily Telegraph 19 September 1908)
© Sheffield Libraries, Archives and Information; Local Studies

The Rev Henry Martin, vicar of St Thomas' Church, Crookes, agreed with the Lord Mayor about expensive funerals and commented on the beauty of the site standing on the summit of the hill and overlooking four beautiful valleys.

The Rev C Ensor Walters, one of the leading Wesleyan ministers in Sheffield, rejoiced at the association of the municipality with the church representatives. He was delighted that there was to be only one Protestant sanctuary and hoped Sheffield would set an example to the country in providing a spirit of unity.

the chapel

Following the opening ceremony, work proceeded on the building of the chapel, details of which can be found in *The Builder 8 October 1910*.

The buildings are executed in Rivelin random coursed walling, hammer-dressed, with dressing of Monk's Park stone for window tracery, doorways, etc and hard gritstone for base and string courses. The chapel roof is covered with the Buttermere Green Slate Company's heavy second slates, the mortuary aisle being roofed with arched ribs and slabs of Stuart's granolithic stone. The interior is groined in cement concrete on ribs of Stuart's stone, with Monk's Park springers and shafts. The church floors have terrazzo and wood flooring and the chancel dove and white marble and steps.

The whole have been carried out from the designs of Messrs C and CM Hadfield, Cairns Chamber, Sheffield by Messrs D O'Neill and Son contractors. Mr C Haywood was the clerk of works.

The interior of the chapel, showing the mortuary aisle (from 'The Builder'). There was just one Protestant chapel, built in a spirit of unity
© Sheffield Libraries, Archives and Information; Local Studies

the layout of the cemetery

The total cost of the chapel, the lodge, laying out the site to harmonise with the main avenue, which had been constructed in 1906 and the boundary walls was £7,395.00.

The cemetery 1909/1910 showing the new mortuary chapel, the main avenue laid out in 1906, the rough land adopted for burial around the chapel and the unadopted land to the east let off as allotments (from 'Picture Sheffield') © Sheffield Libraries, Archives and Information; Local Studies

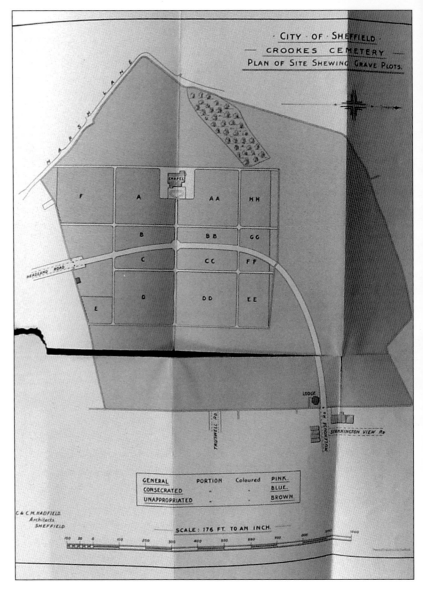

A plan of the cemetery 1910 (from the Rules and Regulations book) showing the proposed sections for burial, consecrated for the church members and general for the non-conformists © Sheffield Libraries, Archives and Information; Local Studies

from the memorial inscriptions...

every grave tells a story

the first burials

Councillor John Maxfield

The first burial in the cemetery was conducted on 3 May 1906 two years before the official opening of Crookes Cemetery. Special permission was obtained from the Home Secretary to allow the burial of Councillor **John Maxfield** who had been instrumental in obtaining the land for the cemetery. His family wished that he should be buried there.

Arrangements were made for the burial to take place. However, the cemetery was at this time merely a field enclosed by a wall with a rough lane leading to it. A group of men worked all night on the Wednesday under the direction of Mr J Platts, Superintendent of City Road Cemetery, to prepare the grave. The land was not yet consecrated, the chapel was still to be built and the walks were still to be laid out. Yet the occasion of a first burial drew much interest and hundreds of people came to offer their last respects.

Evidence of the unity between the non-conformists was seen in that the service took place in St Luke's Wesleyan Church although Councillor Maxfield was a Congregationalist. The service was conducted by Rev TW Holmes, the oldest non-conformist minister in Sheffield and great personal friend of the deceased.

From 'Personal Impressions' (Sheffield Daily Independent 4 May 1906)

Standing by the open grave of John Maxfield, on the windy hilltop at Crookes that will hereafter be a cemetery, but is now little more than a grassy field temporarily broken up here and there for allotments, one felt there was a simplicity in the ceremony, and the surroundings, that fitted well with the modest and genuine man who was being laid to rest. The cemetery is not yet arranged for its ultimate use, nor registered for it, nor consecrated, and this is the first interment – only allowed by special resolution of the 'Burials Sub'; but it was right that it should be, and that hundreds gathered round should remember who it was who was first interred here. The funeral in this place seemed a last link between the dead and the public work he had done. He had been interested in acquiring this land for the City; it is on a hillside where he had so long lived; and it looks forth towards the streams where he had so often taken his quiet pleasure. It may even be that the fact that John Maxfield has been buried here will quicken the action of the City Council, and will lead to the cemetery being more rapidly completed, so that after his death his influence will be tangibly felt. Those of us who worked with him could not escape the inevitable sadness of farewell, made the more touching by the fact that the women of the household had all bravely gathered round the grave; and yet how could man die better? Full of years with a plentiful harvest of usefulness, without long suffering or mental decline, and honoured alike by neighbours and by the City, as the deep ringed crowd of mourners on the hillside showed.

The white Sicilian marble memorial of John Maxfield – the councillor instrumental in obtaining the land for the cemetery and the first interment (Diane Gascoyne 1997)

A monument in white Sicilian marble and of a scroll design was erected in May 1912.

IN MEMORY OF JOHN MAXFIELD
OF THE BOLE HILLS
THIS STONE WAS ERECTED BY MANY FRIENDS
AS A TRIBUTE TO HIS EFFORTS FOR THE MORAL
AND MATERIAL ADVANCEMENT OF HIS FELLOW
CITIZENS, WHOM HE REPRESENTED IN THE
COUNCIL FOR 18 YEARS. HE WAS BURIED IN THIS
CEMETERY BY SPECIAL PERMISSION OF THE CITY
COUNCIL TWO YEARS BEFORE THE OPENING OF
THE CEMETERY FOR BURIALS. AS A PUBLIC MAN
HE HAD HIGH IDEALS, AND FIRMLY BELIEVED IN
THE PRESENT AND FUTURE GREATNESS
OF HIS NATIVE CITY.
'WHERE THERE IS NO VISION THE PEOPLE PERISH'

John Maxfield was head of the firm of J&J Maxfield, silversmiths, in Arundel Street and was a Liberal councillor for eighteen years.

the political botanist, Alfred Russell Fox

On Tuesday 6 December 1910 the Sheffield Daily Independent reported the death of Councillor **Alfred Russell Fox**.

Councillor A Russell Fox, of Crookesmoor Road, had been ill for some time. He had been a capable and unassuming public figure in Sheffield and done much valuable work for the Liberal Party. In the Council Chamber he was known as one of the silent members. He made few speeches but when he did speak it was with brevity and not without influence. Amongst various commitments he sat on the Health Committee and the Education Committee where he was able to improve the welfare of working people.

He was an ardent botanist and did much research into the medicinal properties of plants, being a member of Sheffield Pharmaceutical Society for over thirty years. He was principal partner in the business of his father *William Fox and Sons medical botanists and family chemists* of Castle Street.

He was an enthusiastic traveller and had visited all the principal cities of Europe.

William Fox and Sons, medical botanists and family chemists, Castle Street, Sheffield (extract from Sheffield Local Studies Library material)

The carved cross of the memorial to Councillor Alfred Russell Fox reflects his botanical interest (Diane Gascoyne 1998)

The funeral service was conducted at St John's Wesleyan Church, Crookesmoor by Rev W Percy Hutton. Councillor Fox had been steward and class leader at the chapel and had taken an active part in the men's meetings. Rev Hutton said as Mr Fox's last year had been afflicted with great suffering his Christian faith had been severely tested but he had borne this with patience and bravery. Now there was room to rejoice and give thanks to God for the triumph of his servant. The congregation sang the hymn 'For ever with the Lord' and the service ended with the Dead March in 'Saul'.

the years of World War I

JW Phillips, church organist

On Thursday 13 May 1915 the Sheffield Daily Telegraph reported the death of Mr **John William Phillips** of Wesley Tower, Crookes, the well-known church organist. He was buried in the consecrated section of the cemetery on 17 May 1915, the service being conducted by Rev JT Lewis of St George's Church.

Born into a musical family in 1856 John William was taught by his father Mr Percival Phillips.

A fine grey granite memorial stone erected to JW Phillips by Sheffield Amateur Musical Society 12 July 1916 (Diane Gascoyne 1998)

At only sixteen he was appointed organist and choirmaster of Ecclesall Church and after the death of his father became organist for St George's.

He became accompanist to Sheffield Amateur Musical Society and worked in close harmony with Mr Schollhammer, the conductor, for many years. He was a popular man of modest and retiring nature. He accompanied many well-known singers and also performed recitals in the Sheffield Albert Hall and in many churches.

As an examiner for the Royal College of Music his criticism was candid but kindly.

> ERECTED BY MEMBERS OF THE SHEFFIELD AMATEUR MUSICAL SOCIETY AS A TOKEN OF AFFECTION AND RESPECT AND IN RECOGNITION OF DEVOTED AND TALENTED SERVICE FROM 1877 TO 1915. REQUIESCAT IN PACE

Sadly some people died by accident.

John Bell, admiralty inspector, killed

A fatal accident occurred at Cammell Laird and Co Ltd, Penistone on 16 June 1915. Mr **John Bell**, an Admiralty inspector, was engaged in the inspection of shell material. While passing down the Rail Mill a small bogie came along with an ingot in it. The driver rang his bell but Mr Bell was not able to

The initialled marble cross of John Bell, Admiralty inspector (Diane Gascoyne 1998)

get out of the way and was knocked down and shockingly mutilated. Doctors were quickly on the scene and the Sheffield Motor Ambulance was sent for but death intervened. Mr Bell had only been visiting Penistone for a short while, having taken the place of an Inspector who had gone to America.

Joseph Crapper dies in works accident

On 23 February 1917 thirty-one-year-old **Joseph Crapper** from Hoole Street, Walkley died as a result of an accident at the works of Thomas Firth and Sons, Sheffield. He was admitted to Royal Infirmary with a fractured skull but died some hours later. He had been struck by a heavy crane.

Joseph Crapper accidentally killed at work (Diane Gascoyne 1997)

He is buried in the grave of his in-laws.

. . . ALSO JOSEPH CRAPPER SON IN LAW OF THE ABOVE & BELOVED HUSBAND OF ELEANOR CRAPPER WHO WAS ACCIDENTALLY KILLED AT THOS FIRTH & SONS FEBRUARY 23RD 1917 AGED 31 YEARS . . .

soldiers receive military honours

On 3 January 1917 a military funeral was accorded to Private **John Wilfred Fletcher**, Yorks and Lancs. Private Fletcher of Langsett Road and husband of Mary joined up only seven weeks previously. He died in Lodge Moor Hospital of septic poisoning. Pte Fletcher had been a hairdresser in Dixon Lane before enlisting.

His body was carried to the cemetery on a gun carriage supplied by the Royal Engineers and draped with a Union Jack. Soldiers from Hillsborough Barracks acted as bearers and the chaplain from the Northern General Hospital, Rev FT Cooper, conducted the ceremony.

A military funeral was accorded to Private JW Fletcher, Yorks and Lancs (Diane Gascoyne 2001)

On Saturday 15 September 1917 Private **Arthur Bingham** of the Leicester Regiment was also accorded a military funeral.

The coffin, draped with a Union Jack and surmounted with the deceased soldier's cap and belt, was carried on a gun-carriage provided by the Royal Engineers at Hillsborough Barracks. The service was conducted by Rev GA Hillyar-Russ, from Wesley Hall Methodist Church. Lieutenant Strong MC from Rugely Camp represented the Corps to which Pte Bingham was attached at the time of his death. Pte Bingham lived in Carson Road, Crookes and there was a large and sympathetic gathering of family and friends at the church and the graveside to honour the local man. At the close of the interment trumpeter, Lance-Corporal Baker, sounded the Last Post.

New Cavendish Works, Brookhill, the premises of Westall Richardson, cutlery manufacturer (extract from Sheffield Local Studies Library material)

Mr Westall Richardson, cutlery manufacturer

On Thursday 29 November 1917 the funeral took place of Mr **Westall Richardson**, of Ivy Park Road, Ranmoor. Mr Richardson was a prominent cutlery manufacturer with a business in New Cavendish Cutlery Works, Brookhill, Sheffield where the firm had been established for many years.

The officiating ministers at the funeral were Rev F Holyoake, J Fleming and RT Rowley. Mr Richardson had been a trustee of Broomhill United Methodist Church and representatives were at the funeral. His only son was on military service in France.

RICHARDSON WESTALL, manufacturer of pen, pocket & table cutlery: also hand forge butchers' knives & carvers & stainless cutlery. Cavendish works. Brook hill: h. 78 Ivy Park rd. T.N. 2661

A street directory entry shows the range of cutlery produced (extract from Sheffield Local Studies Library material)

between the wars

Arthur Gratton began work at Crookes Cemetery in 1918 and during his years of service he would have supervised the burials of well-known Sheffield people as well as local residents. He first signed the Burial Register in October 1922 and during that month there were sixteen burials. NF Duncan from St Thomas', SR Butterton from St Nathanael's, George R Ekins from St Timothy's and Oswald Gould presided over thirteen in the consecrated sections of the cemetery and JB Stedeford, J Waldy Skinner, and CE James took the burials in the general parts. All the deceased were from Sheffield and included six people from local hospitals and one from the asylum as well as a two-year-old child and a still-born baby.

The funeral of a child must always have been difficult and some were tragic accidents.

motor fatality

Leslie Slack, son of Albert and Gertude Slack, tragically killed in a motor accident (Diane Gascoyne 2001)

On 1 November 1924 the Sheffield Daily Telegraph reported the death of a six-year-old boy, **Leslie Slack**, from Duncombe Street, who was killed by a runaway lorry in Howard Road, Walkley. The motor lorry laden with coal was proceeding down Howard Hill when the back wheel skidded and the lorry crashed into the wall of a garden. Two small boys were on the pavement and ran in opposite directions as they saw the lorry heading towards them. Slack unfortunately ran into the path of the lorry and was hurled through the wall and on to a shed some five feet below the level of the road. The lorry came to a standstill hanging over the garden shed, which collapsed. The boy was killed instantly.

The driver suffered from shock and was taken to the Royal Hospital. The other child escaped injury. It took some while for the Sheffield Corporation breakdown gang to clear the accident and trams had to run on one track for over an hour.

Rev Arthur Wallace, from St Mary's Walkley, conducted the service.

Charles P Styring, optician

On Tuesday 17 November 1925 the Sheffield Independent reported the death of Mr **Charles Percy Styring** following an operation for appendicitis. He was the proprietor of Lenton and Rusby, opticians, Waingate.

Mr and Mrs Styring named their home in Stumperlowe Crescent Road after the place in France where their eldest son was killed. Gunner **Frank Rusby Styring**, was killed in action at Beaurains in France.

Mr Styring was a key member of St Stephen's Church, Crosspool and did valuable work with the Bible Class and the Young Men's Society but it is for his war work he will be remembered with so much respect.

From the beginning of the war, both he and Mrs Styring were engaged in assisting the wounded men in the City hospitals and in making life easier for the soldiers in camp.

A fine grey granite memorial and a marble cross with a carved Hindenburg tank commemorate Charles P Styring and his son Frank Rusby Styring (Diane Gascoyne 1996)

On the family memorial is a commemoration to their son:

'HE KNEW NO FEAR
HE WAS ONE OF MY BEST MEN
HE WAS GUIDING A TANK OVER THE HINDENBURG
LINE' (OC)
'HE WAS IN THE OPEN POINTING
OUT THE WAY SO THAT HIS CREW
MIGHT GET ALONG SAFELY' (CHAPLAIN)

Mr Styring was president and a pioneer of the Sheffield Branch of the British War Graves Association. He instigated pilgrimages to the Somme battlefield and conducted services at the City Battalion War Memorial in Serre. It was largely through the efforts of Mr Styring that the City Memorial was unveiled on 28 October 1925 in Barker's Pool, Sheffield.

Tommy Ward, entrepreneur

In accordance with a wish expressed during his lifetime, the ashes of Mr **Thomas W Ward** were deposited in Crookes Cemetery 'facing the Rivelin Valley' where he was born. A short service was conducted by Rev Frank Cox.

A funeral service had previously been held on 6 February 1926 in Fulwood Road Wesleyan Chapel, to which members of the Cutlers' Company and Sheffield Chamber of Commerce were invited. Tommy Ward was a prominent figure in Sheffield business circles and in 1913 had been both Master Cutler and President of the Sheffield Chamber of Commerce, a unique achievement.

He was a son of Sheffield, born at Wadsley Bridge. He started work at Walkley Tilt Hammer in the Rivelin Valley at the age of thirteen, where he worked a twelve-hour day starting at four in the morning. Enviously he watched his friends playing cricket whilst he worked. However, he became an entrepreneur starting his own business as a coal and coke merchant at the age of twenty-five. Whilst calling on the cutlers to deliver the fuel he noticed the piles of scrap metal, from which the knife blades had been cut, lying waste and arranged to purchase and remove them. He invented a hydraulic press that crushed the metal into manageable bundles that were easily transported and acceptable to the iron foundries. He became a scrap merchant as well as a coal dealer.

Tommy Ward, entrepreneur, wished for his ashes to be deposited in Crookes Cemetery overlooking the Rivelin Valley where he was born (Diane Gascoyne 1997)

He developed his business by purchasing a small business that made ivory and horn handles for the cutlery trade. His brother Joseph joined him in business. Later, after moving premises, his brother Arthur also joined him.

Ward's empire grew. Whenever any ironworks closed down Tommy Ward was on the spot organising the dismantling and buying the scrap. In the late 1800s at the end of the Sudan War he bought tons of railway lines and formed a railway engineering company. When iron ships were no longer wanted he bought them up for dismantling. At one time he had enough ships to form a navy!

In 1902 he built Albion Works on Savile Street and the business grew from strength to strength. And on his death in 1926 the Ward Group comprised thirty-two undertakings, including engineering firms, quarries, foundries, iron and steel businesses and an interest in the Ketton Cement Company. He secured a lasting place in the Chamber of Commerce by presenting the gold badge, which continued to be worn by succeeding presidents.

He is famously remembered for using Lizzie the elephant to assist with heavy work during WW I, when horses were needed for war work.

A variety of machinery for sale by Thos W Ward, Albion Works, Sheffield (extract from Sheffield Local Studies Library material)

Mr John Banner, businessman

Mr **John Banner** founder and managing director of John Banner Ltd, Attercliffe and a well-known public figure died 17 July 1930, aged 80 years.

John Banner, born in Nottinghamshire and the son of a carrier, began work aged seven years. He came to Sheffield and was successful in business. Banner's department store on Attercliffe was a local landmark and everyone shopped there.

He was a keen Liberal but refused to seek election on the council. He worked in Attercliffe for the cause and was overseer of the poor and also a member of the old Attercliffe Burial Board. In 1901 he became a Guardian for Attercliffe and served for twenty-one years.

John Banner Ltd, Attercliffe, the store where everyone shopped (Diane Gascoyne 1998)

Banners – the house for value with thirty-three departments offering variety and service and up-to-date stock for yourself and your home (extract from Sheffield Local Studies Library material)

For thirty-six years he supported Shortridge Street Methodist New Connexion Chapel but on moving to Beech Hill Road, Broomhill, his allegiance was directed to Broomhill United Methodist Church. He was a trustee and treasurer for many years. The funeral was held at Broomhill Methodist Church and conducted by Rev Norman Green. The report in the Sheffield Daily Telegraph (21 July 1930) lists the attendance of many representatives from the United Methodist Church and from his political and business world. The funeral arrangements were made by John Heath and Sons, funeral directors.

naval honours for ex-Master-at-Arms

In the Telegraph and Star 24 January 1931 there is a report of the funeral of Mr **William Charles Henry Haynes**. Mr Haynes was caretaker of King Edward VII School and an ex-Master-at-Arms of the Royal Navy.

A service was held at St Mark's Church, Broomhill conducted by Rev Harold Ewbank. The coffin was then placed on a gun-carriage, supplied by the Royal Engineers, draped with a Union Jack and covered with wreaths from staff at the school, boys at the school and ex-sevicemen's associations.

A guard of honour was formed by members of Sheffield Naval Branch of the British Legion at both the church and the cemetery. A mounted detachment from the Royal Engineers provided the funeral cortege and the bearers were naval personnel. Mr HJ Revitt sounded the Last Post and Reveille.

the funeral directors

Funeral arrangements for Mr Haynes were by John H Law and Sons, Sidney Street, Moorhead, Sheffield.

Other directors in the 1930s were Joseph Tomlinson and Sons Ltd, the largest funeral furnishers; Reuben Thompson Ltd, complete undertakers and coffin makers; John Heath and Sons, the leading funeral directors, and Brightside and Carbrook Cooperative, Attercliffe Common.

A listing of funeral directors in the 1930s (extract from Sheffield Local Studies Library material)

John Heath and Sons, Earsham Street, Sheffield, funeral directors (extract from Sheffield Local Studies Library material)

Joseph Tomlinson, Bedford Street, Sheffield, funeral furnishers with motor vehicles and horse equipages (extract from Sheffield Local Studies Library material)

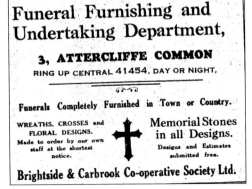

Brightside and Carbrook Cooperative Society Ltd, Attercliffe Common, funeral furnishers and undertakers (extract from Sheffield Local Studies Library material)

A Barker, Brick Street, Crookes, undertaker, joiner and wheelwright (with kind permission of Rita Kettlewell)

In the Parish Magazine for Crookes Church (May 1933) is an advert for the Crookes Undertaker, A Barker, Brick Street.

Quick Press, with branches throughout Sheffield, dyed mourning garments black within twenty-four hours.

Henry Boot, civil engineer

Henry Boot, founder of the world famous firm of Messrs Henry Boot and Sons Ltd, died in his eightieth year at home in Victoria Road on 2 November 1931.

The white marble monument of the Boot family – Henry and his wife Hannah and three of their ten children (Diane Gascoyne 1999)

A service was conducted at the graveside, in accordance with the rites of the Plymouth Brethren in which Henry Boot held a prominent position. The church was overflowing with representatives of the building trade organisations and with members of the Plymouth Brethren from various parts of the country.

The white marble monument was the work of H H Tasker, stonemasons of Abbey Lane.

In this vault are buried Henry Boot 1851-1931, his wife Hannah 1855-1941 and three of their ten children – Gertrude Helen 1873-1935, Ruth Mace 1881-1942 and Edith Annie 1880-1975.

The firm of Henry Boot & Sons is internationally famous for civil engineering and construction work with headquarters at Banner Cross Hall since 1832.

Henry Boot came from a large Sheffield family that originally owned a farm in Heeley. His grandfather, Henry Boot, born 1761, had five sons. William, the eldest, inherited the family farm and was also a stonemason and a shopkeeper. The second son, John, was a publican, the other favoured trade of the Boots.

Charles and Joseph, third and fourth sons, moved across to the other side of the River Sheaf and were working as stonemasons and builders by 1837. Their first building work was probably the houses at Edge Bank where Charles lived. They built the Union Inn in Machon Bank and Joseph moved in. They were then involved with building the Ecclesall Union Workhouse. Joseph combined the trades of stonemason and publican for many years. The youngest son, Henry, kept the Britannia public house in Portobello Street.

William, the eldest son, had two sons, William and Charles. A rift between these brothers resulted in Charles moving over to Sharrow and working as a corn miller. It was his son, Henry, who was to make the name of Boot famous.

Henry served his apprenticeship as a joiner and worked for several Sheffield building firms before he set up his own business in 1886. He built large private houses, public houses and cinemas. His sons, Charles and Edward, joined him in the business and were involved in the building of the triumphal arches erected for the visit of Queen Victoria 1897. They also built the Applied Science Building in Mappin Street for Sheffield University.

During World War I Henry Boot and Sons acquired many Government construction contracts including the Army Camp at Catterick in Yorkshire, Manston Aerodrome in Kent and Calshot Seaplane Base near Southampton. After the war large projects all over the world made the firm internationally famous. When Charles Boot took over from his father as Chairman of the company and moved to the headquarters at Banner Cross Hall in 1932, he would have been able to look out on Brincliffe Edge quarries where his grandfather and great uncle had started their business seventy years earlier.

Tom Mappin, groundsman

In the Deaths column of the Daily Independent 3 August 1932 a notice of interment was given for Mr **Tom Mappin.**

MAPPIN.—At Lindrick, Tom, the dearly beloved husband of Clara Mappin. Interment at Crookes Cemetery, 2.45, August 4th. At rest.

Notice of interment for Tom Mappin, groundsman (extract from Sheffield Local Studies Library material)

The Sheffield Daily Telegraph 5 August 1932 reported on his funeral, which took place 4 August and was led by Rev CP Newell of St Thomas'. Mr Tom Mappin was groundsman of Sheffield and District Golf Club. Members of the Golf Club attended the ceremony.

The memorial of Tom Mappin (Diane Gascoyne 1997)

fatal fall from ladder

William Marsden from Carson Road, Crookes, fell twenty feet to his death. He was working on repairing the slate roof of a house in Arundel Street for his employer George Armitage. As he was about to descend the ladder he was seen to lose his balance and crash head first on to the pavement. He died shortly after admission to the Royal Hospital. A verdict of 'Accidental Death' was returned at the inquest, which followed. Notice of death is mentioned in the parish magazine of St Thomas' and his funeral, led by Rev CP Newell, took place on 8 April 1933.

JW Northend, printer

John William Northend came to Sheffield in 1878 as manager of the printing department of Messrs William Townsend and Sons. In 1889 he began his own business and acquired a reputation for high class work. His colour prints of local moorland scenery were among his notable productions.

JW Northend, printer, Norfolk Row 1909 (extract from Sheffield Local Studies Library material)

Printer, Designer, and Stationer.

IF you entrust your — PRINTING to NORTHENDS you obtain the best return for your money, and get the right kind of work at the right time. The Special Facilities at the . . . . . **New Premises in West Street** ensure Prompt and Efficient Service.

TELEPHONE No. 1432.

JW Northend, printer, designer and stationer, the new premises in West Street 1918 (extract from Sheffield Local Studies Library material)

J.W. Northend Ltd.

Printers and Stationers, 49 West Street, Sheffield

The Sign of Good Printing

SHEFFIELD

Artistic Designers, Catalogue and Pamphlet Specialists, &c.

Printers of the Diocesan Calendar and Official Forms of Service, &c., to be used in the Diocese of Sheffield, by order of The Lord Bishop.

JW Northend Ltd, printers and stationers, West Street Sheffield 1924 (extract from Sheffield Local Studies Library material)

He was a member of the Hunter Archaeological Society from the outset and was the printer for the 'Transactions' illustrating his good taste and craftsmanship.

The son of a professional musician, he was himself an accomplished player. For twenty-five years he played with Sheffield Amateur Musical Society. His love was of chamber music and he played viola in quartet parties on a regular basis.

He and his family were regular worshippers and active members of St Mark's Church in Broomhill. John William Northend was buried 22 December 1933.

The Northend family monument (Diane Gascoyne 1997)

prominent surgeon, Charles Atkin, killed in road accident

Out on his evening stroll on 2 February 1934 Mr **Charles Atkin** was knocked down by a motor car as he crossed the road near Ranmoor Church and received severe head injuries, from which he died before arrival at the Royal Hospital.

Although retired for ten years, Mr Atkin of Endcliffe Vale Road, Fulwood, was a prominent surgeon in Sheffield. He followed his father and grandfather into the profession, after receiving a wide and varied training both in this country and abroad, where he acquired considerable linguistic skills.

He achieved a reputation as a surgeon and for his contributions to the Sheffield School of Medicine and also to the Medical Press. He also acted as referee and examiner for many insurance societies.

On the outbreak of World War I he was about to retire but continued to practise in order that younger men, including his own two sons, could be released for war work.

The stone cross of Charles Atkin FRCS. At present this memorial is dismantled and awaiting reinstatement (Diane Gascoyne 2004)

death of former City fire chief, William Frost

Superintendent **William Frost** died at his Morecambe home aged seventy-four. The funeral and interment took place on 6 September 1938 at Crookes Cemetery. Six members of Sheffield Fire Brigade acted as bearers whilst a guard of honour was formed by other firemen. A wreath of carnations and laurel attached to a fireman's helmet was placed on the grave.

Superintendent of Sheffield Fire Brigade from 1895 William Frost reorganised and remodelled the Brigade to make it one of the smartest and best equipped in the country. When he took up post, attending a fire was the responsibility of the police. Gradually changes were made, until eventually all the latest appliances were at the disposal of a full-time fire brigade.

The fire engines were horse-drawn and William Frost will be remembered for introducing the 'slinging harness', which greatly speeded up the harnessing of the horses to the engines and resulted in a turn out time of 4.4 seconds. During his years in Sheffield, William Frost attended more than five hundred fires and thousands of ambulance cases as the ambulance service was attached to the fire service. He retired in 1915.

Sadly he lost his son, John 'Jack' Frost, in 1918. After following his father into the fire service and serving in Canada he signed up on the outbreak of war but after an accident was sent to England where he joined the Army Service Corps. He developed an illness from which he died aged only twenty-five years.

Superintendent Frost features prominently at the *Fire and Police Museum* at West Bar in Sheffield, his former workplace.

World War II

full military honours for Flying Officer Hemmings

Twenty-four-year-old Flying Officer **William Oliver Chambers Hemmings** was killed in a flying accident near Chichester. He was a member of No 1 Fighter Squadron and would soon have been leader of B flight. Reported in The Star 30 June 1939 is the funeral, which was with full military honours. The service was conducted, at St Mark's, by Canon JWG Gleave. The coffin was borne on an RAF tender and was draped with the Air Ensign. As the cortege entered the church it passed through a guard of honour of airmen

Flying Officer WOC Hemmings, killed in a flying accident, was accorded full military honours (Diane Gascoyne 2002)

standing with reversed arms and officers at the salute. Non-commissioned officers from Finningley acted as bearers and fired a salute over the grave and two buglers from the station sounded the Last Post and Reveille.

Mr AE Boler, commercial artist

The Telegraph and Independent 29 September 1939 reports on the funeral of Mr **Albert Edward Boler** in the presence of a large number of friends and business acquaintances.

Mr Boler of Millhouses Lane was a member of a Balloon Barrage Squadron and died of natural causes while on active service. He was chief artist for Mr Stanley D Dickson, technical advertising expert, and was recognised as one of the most brilliant commercial artists in the Midlands.

An escort party formed by members of his unit met the cortege. The coffin was born by members of the squadron and buglers sounded the Last Post at the graveside. The church service and committal were conducted by Rev JT Hoskins, vicar of St Stephen's and Rev JS Pegge, rector and Rev TEH Baily, curate of Norton.

The Commonwealth War Graves Commission

The Commonwealth War Graves Commission (CWGC) was established in 1917. Its duties are: to mark and maintain the graves of members of Commonwealth forces who died in the two World Wars; build memorials to those who have no known grave; and keep appropriate records and registers.

The registers include civilian as well as military casualties from WWII, some of whom are buried in Crookes Cemetery. The standard CWGC gravestones are a familiar feature of many cemeteries including Crookes and these are kept in excellent condition by CWGC staff.

A Commonwealth War Graves Commission stone marks the grave of Aircraftman AE Boler (Diane Gascoyne 2002)

However, it is less well known that the Commission also undertakes repairs to private family memorials on graves where casualties are buried when they have appropriate permission. A good example of such activity in Crookes is the headstone marking the Snape family grave, where Herbert Snape, who died whilst on leave from Italy in 1918, is buried. In 1999 the headstone lay face down on the ground; in 2002 it was raised and restored by CGWC.

There are several other examples of such work in Crookes Cemetery and the Commission's list of graves in which WWI and WWII casualties are buried totals seventy.

In order to encourage community interest and participation in its work the CWGC introduced a Community Involvement Initiative. Through this scheme, members of the Crookes community check the seventy graves each year and report the condition of each one to the Commission Head Office.

The fallen Snape family gravestone (Diane Gascoyne 1999)

The Snape memorial reinstated by CWGC (Diane Gascoyne 2002)

a woman of vision, Ellen Maud Maxfield

Ellen Maud Maxfield JP, of Bole Hill Cottage, Northfield Avenue, Crookes was the youngest daughter of John Maxfield, who was the first to be buried in Crookes Cemetery. She followed in her father's footsteps working tirelessly for the benefit of the people of Sheffield.

She was a member of Sheffield School Board for forty-five years and then took a place on the Education Committee. A keen educationalist, she spent a lifetime working for the benefit of the children of Sheffield with mental and physical disabilities and was a member of the National Special Schools Union. The 'Maud Maxfield Day School for the Deaf' was first on East Bank Road and then in Ringinglow Road.

She was also a pioneer for women, being a supporter of women's suffrage with a keen interest in work for women. She took an interest in Sharrow House, the Labour Centre's training place for unemployed girls. During World War II, together with Lady Mabel Smith, the selection of land girls was her responsibility. She did knitting and sewing and visited soldiers in hospital. She was one of the few women at the time doing voluntary work as it was considered unwomanly to leave the home.

Her life was one full of service to the community and particularly to those with disabilities. She died 14 February 1940 and is buried with her father.

civilian casualties

In the Parish Magazine of St Thomas's Church, Crookes (January 1941) amongst the list of burials are some casualties from the Sheffield 'Blitz' 12/13 December 1940, including **Horace and Susie Bottom** of Daffodil Road, Firth Park who were killed when their house was bombed. They were subsequently buried in Crookes Cemetery as Horace was the son of Horace and Nellie Bottom of Coombe Road, Crookes, 21 December 1940

Eliza Hall killed in the 'Blitz' 1940
(Diane Gascoyne 1999)

IN
EVER LOVING MEMORY
OF
HORACE
BELOVED HUSBAND OF SUSIE BOTTOM
KILLED THROUGH ENEMY ACTION
DEC 13TH 1940 AGED 44 YEARS
ALSO THE ABOVE NAMED
SUSIE
KILLED THROUGH ENEMY ACTION DEC 13TH 1940
AGED 49 YEARS

by Rev W Todd from St Thomas' Church. Other members of the family are remembered on the memorial inscription including a son missing at Passchendale 1917.

Devonshire Street was also bombed and destroyed on the night of 12/13 December 1940 and **Eliza Hall** aged 88 years was killed.

....
ALSO ELIZA HALL
THE DEARLY BELOVED
MOTHER
OF THE ABOVE
(ISABEL WHEATCROFT)
KILLED BY ENEMY ACTION
DEC 12TH 1940
AGED 88 YEARS

A second wave of bombing on 15 December 1940 resulted in more casualties. In the Sheffield Civic War Dead List is recorded the death of **Ernest Moorhouse**, age forty-two from Bute Street, Crookes, who died on 16 December 1940 in Nether Edge Hospital. Rev W Todd from St Thomas' presided over the burial on 24 December 1940.

Ernest Moorhouse, of Bute Street, killed in a second wave of bombing in 1940 (Diane Gascoyne 1997)

Second Lieutenant George MacBeth

On 21 October 1941, The Star reports that Second Lieutenant **George MacBeth**, a Home Guard officer and William Trevor Wilde, a research worker, were killed when an anti-aircraft shell fell in the road near to them in a North Midlands town. Second Lieutenant MacBeth, a draughtsman, had returned from Home Guard duty and seen that his wife and son were in a safe place before he went out again to do some fire watching.

George MacBeth junior, well known poet and son of the above, later wrote *A Child of the War (published 1987 Jonathan Cape Ltd)* and describes how the news of his father's death was brought to their home. He and his mother were asked to go across the road to the house of friends.

'It probably seemed a long walk for my mother that night. I expect she already guessed why she was going. My memory is of a number of men in the narrow hall and of someone asking me to wait in the front room. Probably someone came in and talked to me. I don't remember.

What I do remember is hearing something I'd never heard before – the sound of my mother crying, somewhere in the distance. Then, a little later, someone came in and said that I had to be a brave boy from now on and look after my mother, because my father was dead.

I don't recall it as being a shock. It was too soon and I was perhaps too young to feel any sense of grief. I went through to the other room and there was my mother and she was crying and she was alive and I sat down beside her, and she put her arms around me and I suppose I tried to say whatever a boy of nine years who has just lost his father tries to say to his mother who has just lost the man she loves.

I didn't cry. I thought it was important not to cry. Boys didn't cry. My father had died and he was a hero, but that wasn't something to cry about.

This all happened over forty-five years ago as I type these lines and things have changed. I haven't struck a single letter without seeing the keys blinded by tears.'

There had been no other deaths that night. No bombs had dropped. An anti-aircraft shell had failed to explode in the sky. It had gone up and then come down in Clarkehouse Road.

Later George MacBeth talks of visiting the grave in Crookes Cemetery:

'My mother and I must have started taking flowers to my father's grave fairly soon. I have memories of the long walk up the hill to Crosspool and then to Crookes where the public cemetery lies on its hill overlooking, now, a valley with much new building.

There was always the valley but in earlier days it was full of trees. I would go through the lines of memorials hunched up in my raglan overcoat or neat and sweating in my school blazer armed with roses or daffodils to remember my father at all seasons, rain or fine, my mother beside me – at first in her dark mourning clothes and later in brighter colours but always tall and beautiful and a little quieter than usual.

There were never tears nor was there ever any talk of my father. We would discuss the weather or the best way to arrange the flowers and then I would help throw away any earlier, withered ones, carrying them in my arms to a tin waste-basket while my mother waited alone at the grave.

What she said or thought or did in those few moments alone I don't know. But there were still no tears when we turned to come away into the wind or the sun, returning through the world of the dead to the shaken and yet not shattered, world of home and school and the network of family and living on.'

© 1987 by George MacBeth, Jonathan Cape Ltd.

The well-known figure of Horatio Bright (extract from Sheffield Local Studies Library material)

some surprises

Horatio Bright

In a cemetery opened in 1908 it is surprising to find a gravestone commemorating people who died in 1891 as is the case with Mary Alice and Sam Bright, the wife and son of Horatio Bright.

Horatio Bright was the son of a well-known jeweller in Waingate. The Bright family were successful and wealthy, renowned for outstanding and meticulous workmanship. Horatio was a traveller for Turton Bros and Mappin at the Old Sheaf Works for many years and married Mary Alice Turton, daughter of Thomas B Turton who had been both Master Cutler and Lord Mayor of Sheffield. Bright set up in business as Turton, Bright and Co, Cross Smithfield, steel manufacturers and was extremely successful. He lived at Lydgate Hall, Crosspool, where he kept many fine horses, a life-long passion. As well as being wealthy he was a fine gentleman, intelligent and gifted with a masterful disposition.

On retirement he renounced his Jewish faith without becoming a Christian and said he wanted nothing to do with religion as far as disposal of his remains was concerned. He wanted his death and burial kept private, with no newspaper reports. He built a private mausoleum at Hollow Meadows, Moscar, called Moscar Rest, near to his summer residence. Here his first wife and their only son were interred without any religious service. When the funeral was arranged for his first wife it was raining so Mr Bright sent the undertakers away to return the following day, if it was fine. Whether this action was out of consideration for his deceased wife or for those attending is unclear. The day was fine and the funeral duly took place.

The Mausoleum was rebuilt in 1906 as it had shown signs of subsiding. When Mr Bright died on 3 February 1906, in respect of his wishes, no one was allowed to know of the funeral. It was arranged for early morning and no one was invited to attend. A reporter from the Sheffield Telegraph found out and was hidden in bushes before it was light on the day. The funeral procession arrived at 8.30am with only the caretaker to provide access. From the first of two coaches was drawn the coffin and from the second came the undertaker and assistants. The men passed into the beautifully decorated mausoleum with family portraits and statues all around. After his first wife's burial an organ was placed in the mausoleum and Horatio Bright played it on his visits.

After the Brights left Lydgate Hall, it remained unoccupied for some years before it was demolished to make way for a housing estate.

The Bright memorial was moved from the private mausoleum at Moscar in 1985 but seems to be missing its original wording 'Horatio Bright who went to sleep on the 3rd of February 1906 in his seventy seventh year' (Diane Gascoyne 1999)

On 7 June 1985 the Bright family's exhumed remains were removed from the mausoleum at Moscar Rest and reburied in Crookes and according to his former wishes without any religious ceremony. The memorial now stands in the general section, truly making the cemetery 'open to all'.

Totley Tunnel commemoration

In 1880 whilst excavating Totley Tunnel members of the Irish community were killed in an accident. There is a small commemorative stone plaque within the cemetery and each year a small service is held in their memory.

a legacy for Sheffield

Sir Stuart Goodwin KB, industrialist and philanthropist

A modest grave reflects a modest man, despite his achievements and works and his many benefactions to the City of Sheffield.

Stuart Coldwell Goodwin was born in Upperthorpe and started work, aged eleven, in the family steel business of Goodwin and Co to get an insight into industry before going away to receive his education. When he returned to Sheffield he joined the family firm. He believed very firmly that hard work produced ample rewards.

However, in 1921 he was stricken with diabetes and was close to death. Only the previous year the properties of insulin had been discovered and Sir Stuart was one of the first people in the country to be able to receive life-saving injections from the Royal Infirmary, which helped him to recovery in less than a year.

It is believed that this dramatic recovery led to his great philanthropic gestures for the City of Sheffield. An almost immediate gift of £10,000 was made to the Royal Infirmary. Gifts continued to be made to a variety of causes in the area of health and education, tradition and sport, all of which benefited the community.

The Goodwin fountain, erected in the Town Hall Square in time for the Christmas illuminations in the 1960s, has now been removed but the Goodwin name lives on – the fountain in the Peace Gardens is named after him.

Sheffield Cathedral is also much indebted to the generosity of Sir Stuart and Lady Goodwin. The extension, the organ and the floodlighting and also the

A fittingly modest headstone for a modest and unassuming man – Sir Stuart Goodwin benefactor of Sheffield (Diane Gascoyne 1996)

restoration of the bells were all made possible by their generosity.

Although he was a man of compassion where it was required, Sir Stuart was himself a man of hard work and action and expected his gifts to help those who were willing to help themselves.

He was essentially an unpretentious man and on the occasion of being made a freeman of the City of Sheffield the Lord Mayor described him as 'being able to make two blades of grass grow where only one had grown before'.

A service took place on 13 June 1969 at Sheffield Cathedral led by ID Neill, Provost of Sheffield, before the funeral cortege made its way to Crookes Cemetery. Sir Stuart had bought a plot many years earlier to ensure he was buried in the city of his birth.

When Crookes Cemetery was opened the speakers were proud that the emphasis was on unity and lack of ostentation. It is therefore fitting that this journey into the lives of the people of Sheffield ends with Sir Stuart Goodwin – a modest and unassuming man.

after 'the war'

The cemetery continued to be a part of life. The children still went to school through the cemetery and the steps opposite the chapel continued to provide the local girls with an impromptu stage and by this time a film set where they could pretend to be Ginger Rogers and dance their way up the sweeping staircase!

'a curtain call' – the local girls line up on the steps opposite the chapel (with kind permission of Thelma Johnson)

the new Superintendent

Michael Grogan took over from Arthur Gratton in 1947. He was a hard worker and very well respected in the district. Mr Egland was in charge of Parks and Cemeteries. Michael had completed his wartime service in the Royal Artillery and on his return had served a couple of years back at Shiregreen Cemetery before he became Superintendent of Crookes.

Electricity had been installed at the Lodge and cables were laid to the Superintendent's office and the chapel during 1948. The beautiful ornate oil lamps which had been in place since the opening of the cemetery were then taken away. A record player was installed with speakers in the chapel to enable suitable hymns to be played during funeral services. As the records were slightly delayed in arriving the equipment was tested one evening using records belonging to Michael's daughter Eileen. These were of the Bing Crosby and Frank Sinatra style!

The family had a one-eyed black cat called Nelson that followed Michael everywhere around the cemetery and used to attend the burial services sitting solemnly at his side with the utmost decorum.

Michael Grogan with his famous cat (with kind permission of the Grogan family)

Michael's family returned from wartime service. His son Paddy and Carmel, his elder daughter, returned to the Lodge from service in the RAF and the Land Army.

All three of his children married from The Lodge in the years that followed, as had Ruth Gratton a while earlier.

Michael's daughter Eileen, with his son Paddy's wife Margaret, on the path outside The Lodge. The allotments where Arthur Gratton grew his vegetables can be seen behind them (with kind permission of the Grogan family)

Michael continued as Superintendent until 1955, signing the Burial Register in his neat hand. He then moved to City Road. The years at Crookes Cemetery and The Lodge had been happy ones for Michael and his family as they had been for Arthur and his family.

By 1962 due to health reasons Michael found the job at City Road too much and applied for a transfer back to Crookes. He had happy memories of Mulehouse Road area and the cemetery was much smaller and more manageable. He was successful in his application and was commuting daily prior to moving house when sadly he suffered a heart attack and died.

Rene Lee came to Stannington View Road in 1952 age thirty-two and remembers a fresh faced Michael Grogan and his two daughters living at The Lodge.

the gravediggers

Her brother **Lou Foster** was a gravedigger in the cemetery and is remembered as a local character. Work started at seven in the morning. Lunchtime was 12.30pm and Lou would walk down to his sister's house for his dinner. His clogs could be heard well before he appeared.

Some parts of the cemetery used to get waterlogged. There were springs under the hillside that eventually caused the land to slip. At one stage the cemetery became very overgrown and dangerous as the graves were breaking up because of the land slipping. Workmen were called in to cut back the grass and tidy things up. Water was always a problem and the graves would fill with water as they were digging or after they had dug them out. Rene remembers seeing a funeral where the coffin submerged under the water as it was lowered into the grave.

Sidney Greatbatch, the father of Ruby Widdowson was also a gravedigger.

After his wife died in 1953 Sid took a job in Crookes Cemetery. He had five children to support and they lived in a terraced house in Stannington View Road.

Ruby was only eleven-years-old when her mother died but she looked after the family and kept house while her family went to work.

Ruby Greatbatch aged ten years, daughter of Sid one of the gravediggers (with kind permission of Ruby Widdowson)

At only thirteen she unwittingly laid a person out. In Stannington View Road people used to accidentally lock themselves out of their houses. When this happened they would send for Ruby. Because she was only small, she could get down the cellar grate and up into the house to let them in. One day when she had done this the woman said quietly, "I think my husband is dead." "Oh we'd better have a look," said practical Ruby. She knew straight away the man was dead and so she straightened his legs and put pennies on his eyes and removed his teeth before he set. These things came naturally to her and when she told her father he said proudly "You did right Ruby."

Sid went to work daily in the cemetery starting at seven in the morning. It was a hard life particularly in the winter. Ruby used to help him wrap his legs in brown paper to keep them warm. Sid lost a thumb in an accident so Ruby used to knit her father mittens to keep his hands warm. He wore clogs and she would hear him coming down the road. His trouser turn-ups were always full of spiders and daddy-long-legs, which he brought into the house. He wore a thick donkey jacket but it was still very cold on the windswept site.

It took three days to dig a grave using a pick and shovel. The deepest grave was for four people. Near the Headland Road entrance at the top of the cemetery there was a hut where the gravediggers used to have their lunch. Ruby used to disapprove of the pin-ups on the wall.

If Sid didn't arrive home for his tea Ruby would have to go and find him. Sometimes, in wet weather, he would get stuck down a grave, as the sides were too slippery to get out. There was a code amongst the gravediggers so that they could find each other. Sid taught his daughter to whistle so that when she was looking for him she would whistle and he would whistle back and she would be able to find him. Then she would put a shovel across the grave so that he could pull himself out.

She would take his meals up into the cemetery if they were busy. The graves had to be ready and the workmen out of the way before the time for the funeral.

When a funeral was arranged Sid used to have to get the boiler going to warm the chapel. Once Ruby found a tramp sheltering in the cellars. She took him food and didn't tell anyone about him but would have been in trouble if she had been found out.

Sometimes the job became a little gruesome. A body takes about twenty years to decompose, the nails and hair keep growing after death. To reopen a grave for a second, third or fourth burial the gravediggers would have to dig down until they hit the board, which was placed across the grave after the coffin had been lowered in. Occasionally the board would be rotten and the gravedigger would go through the wood and through the coffin.

Everyone knew Sid and people used to call at the house and say they thought someone was dying and Ruby would tell them to go for the doctor.

Sid was said to 'dig graves all week and bury veg and flowers at the weekend'. He had an allotment at the side of the cemetery, as did Arthur Gratton. Sid was a member of Crookes Band in his spare time and is remembered for being 'a bit of a character'. He used to comb his hair with soot from the back of the fire to hide the grey hairs.

Sid Greatbatch used to play with Crookes Band (with kind permission of Ruby Widdowson)

approaching the centenary

horse and cart does not come to collect it. The wire baskets for the waste flowers are still there.

Time and the weather have taken their toll on the memorials. The City Council Bereavement Services have made a worthy start on reinstating the memorials and although it will be time consuming and costly, have a programme in place to complete the job, thus maintaining a cemetery which holds a hundred years of Sheffield's history.

'it comes to us all'

the site

In 1908 only part of the cemetery was laid out. The first burials were in sections B, D and DD. By 1916 sections F, A and HH, CC and BB were open. In the 1920s there was need for sections C and EE and GG.

The original plan of the cemetery had to be extended in the 1930s to make full use of the whole site. Section G was opened and section H devoted to Roman Catholics. II and JJ were also opened. During World War II sections LL and KK were opened, with MM and HH1 following in the 1950s. GG1, EE1, I and E have been adopted in more recent times and there are still some plots remaining.

in the 21st century

Crookes Cemetery remains a bright and pleasant place to wander round and read the memorial inscriptions. There are now more than 22,000 interments, with over two hundred war casualty burials and commemorations, seventy of which are looked after by the Commonwealth War Graves Commission.

Today in the 21st century the cemetery still stands high overlooking the Rivelin Valley. Children still go through to Lydgate School. Figures still wander among the graves, visiting and taking flowers or just sitting on the seats.

Burials still take place but there are no longer gravediggers or a Superintendent living close by. The stonemason's workshops are now residences. The greenhouse has gone and although the grass is still cut, the

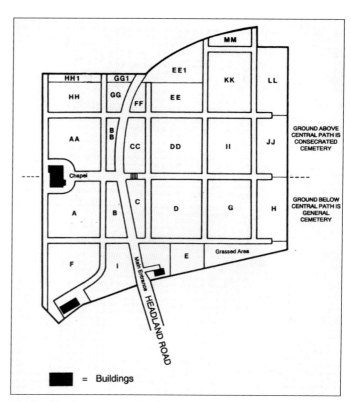

The site of Crookes Cemetery today showing all the adopted sections (with kind permission of Sheffield City Council Bereavement Services)

index of surnames

Ansdell, 6
Armitage, 36
Atkin, 37
Baily, 39
Baker, 29
Ballington, 10
Banner, 32
Barker, 34
Beevers, 21
Bell, 27
Bingham, 3, 8, 15, 29
Birch, 8
Birchenough, 15
Blow, 6
Boler, 38
Boot, 34
Bottom, 40
Bridge, 14
Bright, 42
Butt, 15
Butterton, 14, 18, 29
Butterworth, 9, 13, 14, 18
Comins, 8
Cook, 4, 14
Cooper, 18, 28
Cox, 31
Crapper, 28
Denniff, 7
Dickson, 38
Duncan, 14, 18, 29
Ekins, 14, 18, 29
Elliot, 6

Evans, 15
Ewbank, 33
Firth, 3, 20, 28
Fleming, 29
Fletcher, 28
Foster, 3, 11, 45
Fox, 26
Franks, 15, 18
Frith, 7, 9
Frost, 38
Gascoyne, 14
Gleave, 38
Goodwin, 43
Gould, 29
Gratton, 2, 6, 7
Greatbatch, 45
Green, 33
Grogan, 10, 44
Hadfield, 22
Hall, 40
Hancock 6, 15
Handley, 20
Haynes, 33
Haywood, 23
Heath, 33
Hemmings, 38
Higgins, 15
Hillyar-Russ, 15, 29
Holmes, 25
Holyoake, 29
Hoskins, 39
Hoyland, 11, 15
Hutton, 27

James, 17, 29
Kemp, 21
Kettlewell, 7, 20
Knowles, 17, 22
Law, 33
Lee, 45
Lenton, 30
Lewis, 27
Lister, 7
MacBeth, 41
Mappin, 35, 42
Marsden, 36
Marsh, 4, 22
Martin, 14, 23
Matthews, 14
Maxfield, 25, 40
Mills, 3
Moorhouse, 40
Motson, 8
Neill, 43
Newell, 5, 21, 36
Northend, 36
O'Neill, 23
Oxley, 18
Paterson, 8
Pegge, 39
Phillips, 27
Platts, 25
Pratt, 4
Reaney, 6
Revitt, 33
Richardson, 29
Rowley, 29

Rusby, 30
Sadler, 9
Sanderson, 7
Schollhammer, 27
Senior, 22
Skinner, 29
Slack, 30
Smith, 18, 40
Snape, 39
Spencer, 15
Stead, 8
Stedeford, 29
Stephenson, 4
Strong, 29
Styring, 30
Tasker, 35
Thompson, 33
Todd, 40
Tomlinson, 33
Townsend, 36
Turton, 42
Twigge, 7
Tyler, 6, 9, 15
Wagstaffe, 21
Wallace, 30
Walters, 14, 23
Ward, 31
Widdowson, 45
Wilde, 41
Wright, 15

further research

Sheffield Archives, Shoreham Street, Sheffield, holds Crookes Cemetery Burial Register on microfilm with an index.

Sheffield Local Studies Library, Surrey Street, Sheffield holds local newspapers on film.

Photographs and further information about some of the places mentioned in this book can be found in:

Crosspool *by Judith Hanson, Tempus Publishing Ltd;*

Central Sheffield *by Martin Olive, Tempus Publishing;*

A Second Helping of Peter Harvey's Sheffield, *Sheaf Publishing;*

Crookes Revisited, *Crookes Local History Group;*

'They Lived in Sharrow and Nether Edge', *by Nether Edge Neighbourhood Group;*

Banner Cross Hall, *by I R Baines*

A History of JW Northend Ltd printers of Sheffield, *by Roy Millington*

Sheffield and District Family History Society provides help with researching family names and places.